Kansas State Capitol
Topeka

Jane Moorman

There is a saying, "It was a Friday night and it seemed like a good idea at the time." That sums up the beginning of the State Capitols Project.

When I told my brother of my idea of photographing state capitols, he said, "You do know there are 50 states and two of them you can't drive to."

Each capitol has its own unique beauty that reflects the state's personality when it was built.

Jane Moorman, photographer

Kansas Statehouse: Reflects Historical Past

When Kansas became a U.S. territory in 1854, federal law specified that the citizens of the new territory should decide the issue of slavery for themselves.

Advocates for and against slavery converged on the new territory during a period known as Bleeding Kansas.

Constitutions advocating pro and anti-slavery were written by special interest groups.

After rejecting the document that would allow slavery, the voters approved the state constitution that forbade slavery in the state. This allowed Kansas to receive statehood in 1861.

Kansas had only been a state for five years when construction on its capitol began in 1866. But it took 37 years to complete the structure.

The first legislature approved the capitol designed by architect E. Townsend Mix of Mil- waukee, Wisconsin, and modified by John G. Haskell of Lawrence, Kansas. Other architects were involved with the project during construction.

When the original soft sand stone foundation deteriorated quickly, it had to be rebuilt with Kansas limestone delaying the completion of the first stage until 1873.

Work on the west wing began in 1879 and was occupied in 1880. The central section with the towering dome was authorized in 1881, with work beginning in 1885. All structural work was finished by 1903.

The state's leaders wanted the European Renaissance Revival architectural style to reflect their pride in Kansas' stormy path to statehood and their grand hopes for its future. Throughout the interior of the capitol many types of marble are used: Tennessee and Georgian marble, Siena and Lambertin marble from Italy,

Numidian marble from Africa, and Royal marble from France. Throughout the interior columns and stairways are polished copper. The surface of the exteriordome is, also, copper.

First Dome Statue

Ceres, the Roman goddess of agriculture, by artist J.H. Mahoney was selected in 1889 to top the dome.

The proposed 16-foot bronze statue was rejected and the dome remained unadorned until the installation of Ad Astra in 2002.

Copper Dome

The Kansas capitol is crowned with a copper dome. The top is 306 feet above the ground. Round windows allow light to enter the area around the interior dome to illuminate the rotunda.

Ad Astra

The Kansa warrior Ad Astra was placed on top of the dome in 2002. Sculpted by Kansas artist Richard Bergen, it is 22 feet and 2 inches tall and weighs 4,420 pounds. The statue is named for the state motto: Ad astra per aspera, "To the stars through difficulties."

Rotunda Dome

Glass panels illuminate the copper columns and curved walls that support the dome. The 10-foot by 10-foot chandelier is identical to the one in the capitol's House of Representatives chamber.

Rotunda From Above

Visitors to the capitol who tour the dome have a view of all seven floors of the rotunda from the seventh floor balcony.

Between The Domes

A once-a-day tour to the top of the dome allows visitors to enter the space between the inner and exterior dome.

From the fifth floor, they climb 296 steps to reach the base of the cupola outdoors.

The top of the rotunda dome is 75 feet from the cupola floor.

A winch is permanenly attached to the rotunda dome to lower the chandelier for cleaing.

Light from the exterior dome windows illuminates the rotunda through glass panels, forming the inner dome.

Dome Murals

Abner Crossman of Chicago created four allegorical murals for the rotunda dome in 1902. Each scene was done on canvas and cut and fitted onto the curved surface.

Plenty in the center with Labor on her left and Agriculture on her right.

Power in the center with a Spanish-American War solider and a Civil War Union solider.

Knowledge in the center with Temperance on her left and Religion on her right

Peace in the center with Science on her left and Art on her right.

Copper Staircases

Ceremonial Office

The former Secretary of State's office is now used as a ceremonial office site.

Senate Chamber

House of Representatives Chamber

John Steuart Curry Murals
Kansas Pastoral

John Steuart Curry's "Kansas Pastoral" mural depicts a farmer and his wife standing in front of their farmhouse and barn. Each mural contains symbols of Kansas industries—agriculture and oil.

Tragic Prelude

John Steuart Curry's Tragic Prelude, considered among the best public art, features abolitionist John Brown with outstretched hands containing the Bible in his left and the 'Beecher's Bible' in his right. Beside him, facing each other are contending free soil and pro-slavery forces. He stands on the bodies of Union and Confederate soldiers. On each end of the mural is a tornado and prairie fires to represent the gathering storms of war. Curry's work was controversial at the time he created it. Critics at the time disliked the over-all menacing effect of the mural. Because of the strained relationship, Curry refused to sign his work.

Lumen Martin Winter Murals

The artwork on the second floor of the rotunda was painted by Lumen Martin Winter in 1978.

The native of Larned, Kansas, painted the scenes with oil on canvas. He used the walls' structure to create a three-dimensional effect.

Overmyer Murals

David H. Overmyer's murals on the first floor significant events in Kansas history, from the Spanish explorers to the westward migration of future Kansas residents. In 1953, the Topeka resident painted directly onto the plaster wall.

Coming of the Spaniards

Lewis and Clark in Kansas

Battle of Mine Creek

The Chisholm Trail

Battle of Arkikaree

Westward Ho

Building a Sod House

Arrival of the Railroads

Brown v. Board of Education Mural

The Brown v. Board of Education mural by artist Michael Young of Kansas City, created in 2018, depicts the legacy of the 1954 landmark U.S. Supreme Court desegregation case, with roots in Topeka. The mural is located outside the old state supreme court chamber where earlier civil rights cases were fought, leading the way to a turning point in the history of the United States.

We The People

The Kansas Chapter of the Veterans of Foreign Wars donated these stained-glass windows in 1976 in celebration of the 200th anniversary of the founding of the United States. The banners state "With Liberty and Justice For All" and "Honor the Dead by Helping the Living."

From Bygone Years

Installed in 1923, the hand-operated 'cage' elevator and a shoe-shine stand chair are unique by today's standards.

In 1976, the legislature determined the elevator to be of historical value and resolved it to be maintained in operating condition.

Kansas State Seal

The Seal of Kansas and the state motto, "Ad astra per aspera" were adopted by the first Kansas legislative session on May 25, 1861.

"Ad astra per aspera" motto, meaning "To the stars through difficulty," is at the top of the seal.

Below the motto are 34 stars representing Kansas' entry as the 34th state in the Union.

The symbolism of the figures on the seal are as follows:

The east is represented by a rising sun in the right-hand corner of the seal; to the left of it, commerce is represented by a river and a steamboat; in the foreground, agriculture is represented as the basis of the future prosperity of the state by a settler's cabin and a man plowing with a pair of horses; beyond this is a train of ox-wagons going west; in the background is a herd of buffalos, retreating, pursue by two Native Americans on horseback.

When the seal is used by the governor of Kansas, the circle is surrounded by the words, "Great Seal of the State of Kansas, January 29, 1861."

A color version of the Seal of Kansas is found on the wall entering the Senate chamber.

About the Photographer

Jane Moorman describes herself as an adventurer who loves to drive backroads to see what there is to see.

During her 30-year journalism career, Jane honed her photograpic skills as a photojournalist including covering high school sporting events.

A friend once said, "I wish I could see the world as Jane sees it. Finding the beauty in things that most of us don't take time to see."

Upon retiring in 2021, Jane decided there is a lot of her native country she had not visited, so she began her journey of exploring the USA.

She currently lives in Albuquerque, New Mexico, but says her real home is on the road.